18554ul

Uncle Pete the Pirate

Susannah Leigh
Designed and Illustrated
by Brenda Haw

Editor: Karen Dolby
Assistant Editor: Michelle Bates
Series Editor: Gaby Waters

Contents

About this Book

MARY

UNCLE PETE

Keep your eyes open for clues. If you get stuck, there are answers on pages 31 and 32.

When this book begins, Mary is looking forward to her Uncle Pete the pirate, coming to visit. Uncle Pete comes home once a year and this time he has the most amazing pirate adventure in store for Mary. Just turn the page to find out more...

Uncle Pete Arrives

On the day Uncle Pete came to visit, Mary raced down to the little port near her house where she had promised to meet him. Mary couldn't wait to see Uncle Pete again. She wondered if he would be wearing his blue pirate hat. He was sure to have some pirate tales to tell, if only she could find him.

Can you see Uncle Pete?

Funfair Today

4

5

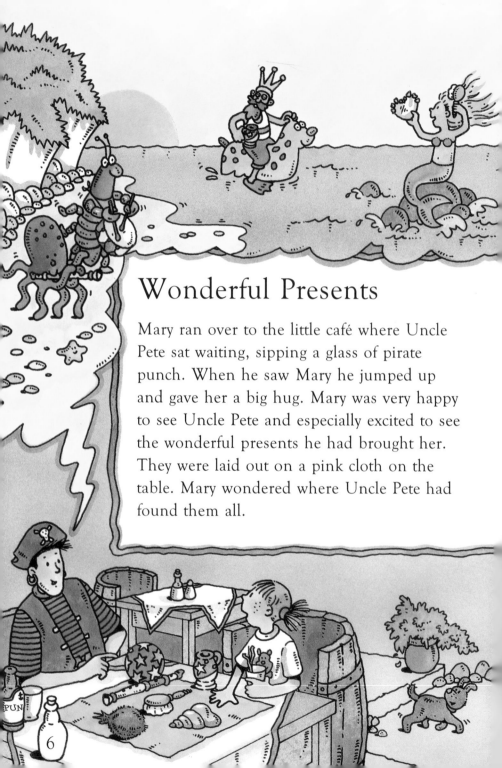

Wonderful Presents

Mary ran over to the little café where Uncle
Pete sat waiting, sipping a glass of pirate
punch. When he saw Mary he jumped up
and gave her a big hug. Mary was very happy
to see Uncle Pete and especially excited to see
the wonderful presents he had brought her.
They were laid out on a pink cloth on the
table. Mary wondered where Uncle Pete had
found them all.

"Your presents came from the friends I made during my adventures at sea," he said.

Uncle Pete told Mary about all the fantastic places he had been to and all the amazing things he had seen on his pirate journey. His story was so real, she could picture him sailing across the ocean. She could even guess exactly where each of her presents came from.

Can you guess where Uncle Pete found each of Mary's presents?

Pirate Surprises

Uncle Pete and Mary walked back up the road to
Mary's house.

"I hope you won't be bored, Uncle Pete," Mary
sighed. "Nothing piratey ever happens here."

Uncle Pete just smiled. He was sure Mary was in
for a surprise.

"I think your house is a pirate's playground, Mary," he said. "Look closely and see for yourself."

Mary rubbed her eyes. She gasped with delight. She rubbed her eyes again, but there was no mistake. Today her house looked very piratey indeed.

Can you spot any pirate things at Mary's house?

A Mysterious Message

Mary shivered with excitement and grinned at Uncle Pete. She had a feeling a pirate adventure was just around the corner. She was even more sure when they stepped inside the house and Uncle Pete handed her a postcard. "I found this on the doorstep, Mary," he said. "It's addressed to you. It seems to be some sort of picture message. I wonder what it says."

What does the card tell Mary to do?

Dear Mary
go to this 🧰
and find a 📜
from a well-wisher ☠

Dear
gone
will look
after you
love

11

Treasure Map

This map belongs to Bad Luck Barry
who stole a chest of treasure rare.
That chest was full and hard to carry,
so Barry hid it – over there.

"Over there? Where's that? Please tell."
One picture on this map will show
Barry, burying that treasure well.
Where's it hidden? Do you know?

Saucepan Island

School House

Aunty Brenda's House

Sandcastle Island

Puppy Island

Sure enough, on top of the chest, Mary found a rolled up
piece of paper. She spread it out. It had pictures and a
short poem written on it. Uncle Pete read the poem and
gave a great shout.

"Shivering shipwrecks, Mary!" he cried. "This is a
treasure map. It belongs to the pirate Bad Luck Barry."

A pirate's treasure map! Mary could hardly believe it. Eagerly she read Barry's poem. She looked at the pictures and caught her breath. "Uncle Pete," she exclaimed. "I can see where Barry buried the treasure!"

Can you see where the treasure is buried?

13

Uncle Pete Explains

The map showed Bad Luck Barry burying the treasure on Lawnmower Island. But Mary was still puzzled. There were lots of things she didn't understand. Who WAS Bad Luck Barry? Where was Lawnmower Island? And what was the treasure buried there? Uncle Pete explained.

Bad Luck Barry is my oldest pirate enemy.

He stole my precious treasure chest.

Then he hid it on Lawnmower Island, which isn't far from here. We must watch out for Barry. He may be very near...

14

Mary shivered. What an exciting story! She wondered where Barry could be now.

Can you see him?

15

Ship Ahoy!

"When Barry realizes his map is missing, he will be very angry," said Uncle Pete. "We must sail to Lawnmower Island and find my treasure, but first we'll need a pirate boat. Let's see if we can spot one from your roof, Mary."

They scrambled up the ladder to the roof where they could see for miles around. Mary looked down over the large garden. "I can see a perfect boat, Uncle Pete," she cried.

Can you see what Mary and Uncle Pete can use as a pirate boat?

17

Puzzling Parrots

Mary and Pete jumped aboard their pirate boat and set sail.

They passed fields and trees, cows who said "moo" and fish who flew.

Mary saw other pirates
. . . and waved to friends.
All of a sudden, two pirate
parrots on perches squawked
out a message in rhyme.

You're on the right trail,
but how do we know?
Some things have been pointing
the right way to go.
On Lawnmower Island these
same things will tell,
the way to the treasure,
so follow them well.

Mary giggled. How funny to hear
parrots talking. She scratched her head and
wondered what their strange message meant.

**What things have been pointing the way
on the river journey?**

19

Juicy Jellyfish

Uncle Pete peered through his treasure-hunting telescope.
"Land Ahoy!" he said. "Drop anchor, Mary. Lawnmower
Island is dead ahead."

Lawnmower Island! Mary quivered with excitement.
Would they really find the treasure here? Uncle Pete tied up
the boat and Mary splashed through the shallow water.
Almost at once she saw the blue arrow that pointed them to
the right path. Mary ran toward the island's soft warm sand
when a shout from Uncle Pete stopped her.

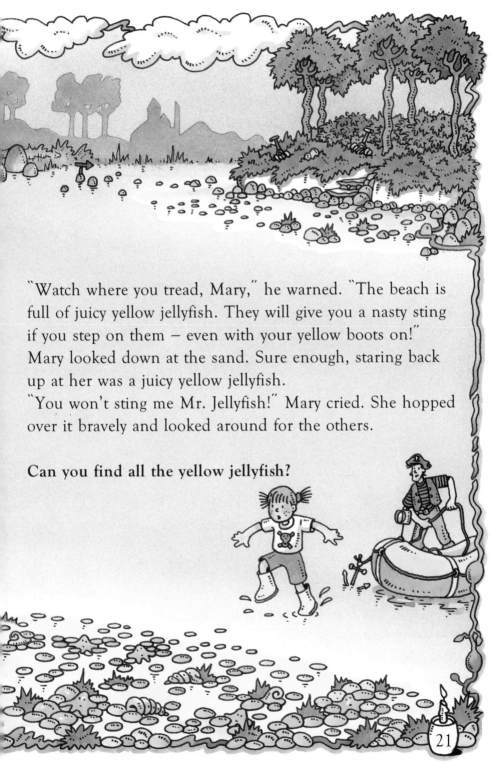

"Watch where you tread, Mary," he warned. "The beach is full of juicy yellow jellyfish. They will give you a nasty sting if you step on them – even with your yellow boots on!" Mary looked down at the sand. Sure enough, staring back up at her was a juicy yellow jellyfish.

"You won't sting me Mr. Jellyfish!" Mary cried. She hopped over it bravely and looked around for the others.

Can you find all the yellow jellyfish?

Wild Beast!

Mary and Pete skipped past the last yellow jellyfish and followed the blue arrow that pointed them deeper into the dark and tangled jungle and closer to Uncle Pete's lost treasure.

Mary looked back to make sure that Uncle Pete was following close behind, when a loud roar stopped her in her tracks. Mary gulped and turned around slowly. She found herself face to face with a large, hairy beast. It had very sharp teeth and big ears.

"Fiery fishtales, Mary!" cried Uncle Pete. "It's the wild beast of Lawnmower Island. If we can find some tasty bones to feed it with, we will be able to sneak past it safely."

Can you find seven bones for the wild beast to munch?

Slimy Stones

The wild beast snuffled off with a mouthful of bones. Mary held tightly to Uncle Pete's hand as they continued following the blue arrows across the island. They stopped at a deep pool of water and Pete shook his head. There was no way around. They would have to cross by the stepping stones. Mary sighed. First jellyfish, then a wild beast and now this.

Being a pirate was hard work. You never knew what was just around the corner. But Mary was brave, she wouldn't give up yet. So she jumped from stone to stone, being careful not to tread on the slime and the toads.

Can you find a way across the stepping stones to the blue arrow on the other side of the water?

Pirate Treasure

Mary jumped from the last stepping stone
and crashed on through the jungle. As she turned a
corner she gasped. What do you think she saw? There,
sitting in the middle of Lawnmower Island on a checked
blanket, were her mother and father!

"Surprise, Mary," they cried. "You're almost at the end
of the trail. Take this spade and dig here for the pirate
treasure."

Mary turned to Uncle Pete who smiled broadly. Mary
grinned and began to dig. Before long she hit something
hard. With Uncle Pete's help, she lifted the object
from the ground. It was a treasure chest.

Inside was the most wonderful pirate picnic Mary had ever seen.

"Eat up Mary," said her dad, brushing the sand from the sandwiches. "And tell us all about your pirate adventures."

Mary was just about to munch on a piece of a pirate pie and tell them all about her exciting time, when she had a terrible thought. Where was Bad Luck Barry? He was sure to be somewhere near and he would want the treasure...

Bad Luck Barry won't want any treasure and he won't be troubling Mary. Can you see why?

Goodbye Uncle Pete

After everyone had eaten enough, they sailed
back to Mary's house. Then Uncle Pete had
to leave. That evening Mary went down to the
little port to see him off. She wanted to say
one last goodbye and thank him for her
marvellous pirate adventure. There was a
funfair at the port. But where
was Uncle Pete?

Can you see him?

GHOST TRAIN

BUGGY RIDE

Have
Fun!

FUNFAIR

TODAY
ONLY!

BALLS A
FLUTES —
EVERY

UNCLE PETE'S PIRATE RIDE

COCONUT SHY

29

Funfair

"Climb aboard, Mary," Uncle Pete called from the pirate ride. Mary scrambled up and clung on tightly as the merry go round whirled and spun. The wind whistled through her hair and music played loudly.

"I'll be back to visit you next year, Mary!" Uncle Pete called above the noise of the fair. "Would you like that?"

Mary thought about her wonderful day. "Oh, yes please, Uncle Pete," she cried. "This has been the best pirate adventure I have ever had!"

Answers

Uncle Pete has one more puzzle for you. How many lawn mowers can you find on Lawnmower Island?

Pages 4-5
Uncle Pete is here.

Pages 6-7
Uncle Pete tells some exciting stories! Here is where Uncle Pete says he found each of Mary's presents. The octopus gave him the flute and the king gave him the cup. The brush belonged to the mermaid and the monkey threw Uncle Pete a coconut. Neptune gave Uncle Pete a listening shell, and the ball is the one the dolphins are playing with.

Pages 8-9
The pirate things at Mary's house are circled in this picture.

Pages 10-11
The card tells Mary to go to this chest

and find this map. (Did you spot the other picture message here?) It says: Dear Mary, Gone fishing. Uncle Pete will look after you. Love Ma and Pa.

Pages 12-13
The treasure is buried on Lawnmower Island. Here is Bad Luck Barry hiding it.

Pages 14-15
Barry is here.

Pages 16-17
Mary has spotted a rubber dinghy which they can use as a pirate boat. Here it is.

Pages 18-19

The blue arrows have been poiting the right way to go. They are circled here.

Pages 20-21

You can see the eleven jellyfish that Mary has to watch out for circled here.

Pages 22-23

The seven juicy bones are circled here.

Pages 24-25

The way across the stepping stones to the blue arrow is marked in black.

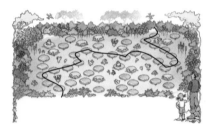

Pages 26-27

Bad Luck Barry won't want any treasure because he is really a scarecrow! Here he is.

(Did you spot him on page 17 being carried by the farmer?)

Pages 28-29

Uncle Pete is here. Did you guess?

(Can you see some familiar presents here?)

There are ten lawn mowers on Lawnmower Island.

This edition first published in 2002 by Usborne Publishing Ltd., Usborne House, 83-85 Saffron Hill, London EC1N 8RT, England. www.usborne.com Copyright © 2002, 1994 Usborne Publishing Ltd. The name Usborne and the devices are Trade Marks of Usborne Publishing Ltd.

Printed in South China.
This edition first printed in America 2003. UE

J 12-05
c.2